Journey
Through a
Tropical Jungle

BY ADRIAN FORSYTH
WITH AN AFTERWORD BY HRH PRINCE PHILIP, THE DUKE OF EDINBURGH

Simon and Schuster Books for Young Readers
Published by Simon & Schuster Inc., New York

SIMON AND SCHUSTER
BOOKS FOR YOUNG READERS
Simon & Schuster Building
Rockefeller Center
1230 Avenue of the Americas
New York, New York 10020

Text copyright © 1988 by Adrian Forsyth

Photographs used with permission:
André Bärtschi: page 30 *center,* 58 *center;* Michael Fogden: page 7 *right,* 8, 9, 20, 24 *center,*
26 *left,* 28, 29, 30 *left,* 33 *right,* 34, 35 *top right,* 40, 41 *top right,* 42 *top left,* 43 *right,*
47 *right,* 57 *right,* 66 *left,* 70 *center,* 72 *center,* back cover; Michael and Patricia Fogden: page 19 *right,* 32 *center,*
38 *center,* 43 *bottom left,* 46, 50, 51, 52, 53, 54, 59 *right,* 60 *top right,* 60 *center,*
64 *center,* 67 *bottom right,* 68 *right,* 74 *right;* Turid Forsyth: page 6 *left,* 25 *right,* 39 *right,* 45 *right,*
55 *right,* 64 *right;* Richard Laval: page 24 *left;* Bruce Lyon: page 10 *center,* 11, 16 *center,* 18 *center,*
21 *left,* 26 *center,* 27, 31 *right,* 34 *right,* 36; Michael Fogden/Animals Animals: front cover.

All other photographs copyright © 1988 Adrian Forsyth

Originally published in Canada by Greey de Pencier Books, Toronto.

SIMON AND SCHUSTER BOOKS FOR YOUNG READERS
is a trademark of Simon & Schuster Inc.

Designed by Wycliffe Smith
Map by Tony Delitala
Illustrations by Julie Wootten

Manufactured in Hong Kong

10   9   8   7   6   5   4   3   2   1

Library of Congress Cataloging-in-Publication Data

Forsyth, Adrian.
Journey through a tropical jungle/by Adrian Forsyth.
Includes index.
Summary: Presents in text and photographs some of the plants, animals, and people
that live in the tropical rain forest of Costa Rica.
1. Rain forest ecology—Costa Rica—Juvenile literature. 2. Rain forests—Costa Rica—Juvenile literature.
[1. Rain forest ecology—Costa Rica. 2. Rain forests—Costa Rica. 3. Ecology.] I. Title.
QH541.5.R27F68 1989   574.5′2642′09728—dc 19   88-14683   CIP   AC

ISBN 0-671-66262-7

Contents

Introduction

Tropical forests are the richest places on our planet. But the riches they contain are not gold or silver or diamonds: they are rich in life. Although tropical forest covers only 6 percent of the Earth's surface, it is home to two-thirds of all the species of plants and animals on our planet. These plants and animals are now threatened with rapid extinction. In just the past 100 years half of the world's tropical rain forests have been razed to the ground for the lumber they contain, and to make way for farmland. The birds, the orchids, the butterflies, the monkeys — all the animals and plants that depend on these jungles are being destroyed by logging, burning and bulldozing. The remaining half of the world's tropical forests are under growing pressure. About 20 hectares (50 acres) a minute are being destroyed — that's an area of tropical forest almost as large as England every year. As a biologist I wanted to see these fantastic forests and the wildlife they contain before they disappear. I set out to visit Costa Rica, a tiny Central American country that is working hard to protect as much of its jungles as it can. My trip could only last a few short weeks, but I knew those weeks would be filled with wonder.

The Route

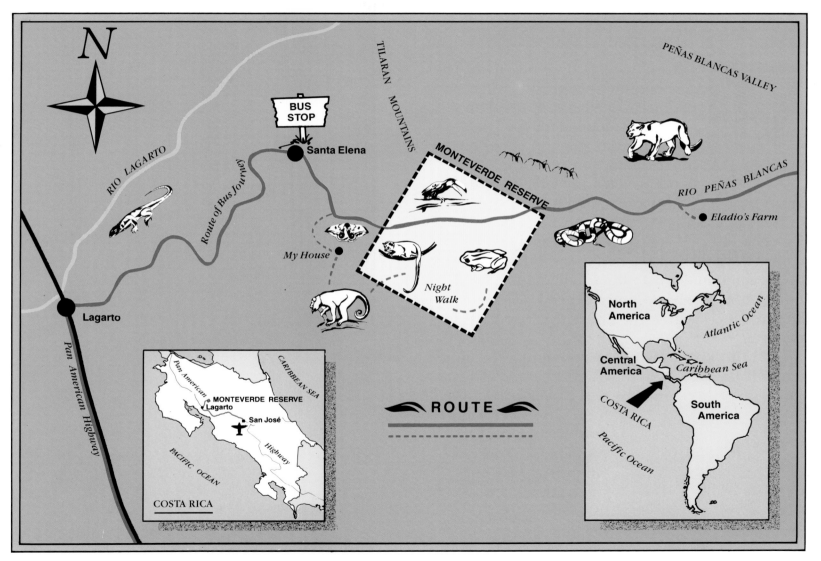

End of the Road

My stop! I whistled to the driver. The air brakes wheezed and puffed as the bus slowed and stopped on a steep hill. I hauled my backpack down the bus steps and jumped out into brilliant sunshine.

I was standing at Kilometer 149 on the Pan American Highway in Costa Rica. A sleepy brown pig was there to greet me. It looked up from its siesta, snorted and closed its eyes again. "Welcome to Lagarto," it seemed to say. Lizardville, you might call it in English. Lagarto was a small collection of houses, shacks and a general store named after the Rio Lagarto, the Lizard River, which ran nearby.

It looked shady and cool under the huge umbrella-shaped trees down by the river, so I wan-

dered over for a closer look. This river was a kind of signpost for me. The Rio Lagarto wound its way in the same direction as the first leg of my journey.

Upstream were the Tilaran Mountains, part of the backbone of mountains extending from the Canadian Rockies all the way down through Central America. Another bus would take me up through the dry foothills on the Pacific slope of these mountains until I reached their wet, windy top. Then my trail would go downhill through the lush rain forests coating the Atlantic slopes of the mountains. Along the way I hoped to discover many strange and beautiful tropical plants and animals.

Right away I saw something strange by the river. A huge lizard, as big as a large dog, waddled along the ground. I thought, "Perhaps this is how the river got its name." It was a male ctenosaur (pronounced *teen-o-sor*) lizard looking like something out of the Dinosaur Age. He had scaly skin banded with stripes of blue-gray and black and a huge spiny crested head with a very wide mouth.

He was tilting his head up and down again and again. The cause of all this head-bobbing was another ctenosaur nearby, who was also head-bobbing. Each was signaling that this was his territory: "Keep out, no trespassing." But it soon became clear that both lizards would rather feed than fight. As I watched, they put their heads down and began to pull up large mouthfuls of weeds.

Mature ctenosaurs are vegetarians. They are the cows of the lizard world. They begin life as small, lively green lizards that race through the grass and eat insects. They will even wait by a porch lamp to snag the moths and other insects that are attracted to the light. When they are middle-aged, about three years old, they can still catch the odd mouse or frog. But at full size, when they have turned blue-gray, they have become too slow to catch much more than leaves and flowers.

When they finally noticed me, both ctenosaurs scrambled up a cashew tree. This was understandable. Not only do snakes and hawks enjoy a meal of ctenosaur, people here also eat these lizards. Each year thousands of ctenosaurs are sold in rural Central American markets. However, the habit is dying out because it is considered old-fashioned to eat lizard meat and because the forests that these lizards depend on are rapidly being destroyed.

As I strolled along the riverbank I heard loud quacking noises overhead. It sounded as though the treetops were filled with ducks. Looking up I saw birds unlike any I had ever seen before. They had huge black eyes and very wide bills. I had read about birds like this: I had found a group of boat-billed herons. All the quacking was because I had disturbed their daily sleep. These herons feed at night. They stand in the river and use their wide eyes and bills to catch fish and insects in the water.

The quacking disturbed another animal sleeping in the tree. I saw an iguana lizard, as large as a ctenosaur, scrambling along a branch reaching over the river. The iguana had been so well camouflaged by his greenish skin that I didn't see him until he reached the end of the branch.

The lizard fell off like a stone, belly-flopping with a huge splash into the river, and then swam away under water. It wasn't a graceful exit but it was effective.

I decided to make my own exit from Lagarto. Even though the bus that would take me up the mountain was due soon in Lagarto, I wanted a close-up look at the foothills. I shouldered my pack and began trudging along the gravel road leading up toward the cloud-wrapped mountains in the distance.

The road was bordered by "naked Indian" trees, so named for their reddish-brown bark, which looks like skin. There were also rows of hog plums. These trees were being used as living fence posts to support barbed-wire fencing. The bright red fruit tasted delicious, like tart cherries. As I walked along, chewing the fruit and spitting out seeds, I realized the trees not only provide a never-ending supply of firewood or new fence posts for farmers, they also supply food and nesting places for birds and other wildlife.

Unfortunately, these roadside trees were throwing no shade. Unlike our trees, they shed their leaves in summer!

Costa Ricans call their dry season summer and their wet season winter. In summer, which begins in December, there is no rain for months in the plains and lowlands. People can go to the beach to get wet and cool, but the trees are stuck with a problem. Their leaves lose large amounts of water through evaporation, as much as 225 litres (60 gallons) of water every hour from just one tree. So to keep from drying out, the trees in the dry regions simply drop their leaves and stand bare until just before the rains start in May.

A landscape of pastures and bare trees sounds bleak, but it was actually colorful. Many trees were bursting into flower. As I trudged along I saw one completely coated in large purple flowers and others decked out in bright yellow. Bees were busy making honey and I could hear their hum in the still air.

With no wind and no shade, sweat was pouring off my forehead. The droplets made muddy streaks in the road dust coating my face. It was just too hot to be out in the sun. My only companions were the tiny doves that flushed up from the roadside and then settled in the grasses to watch my slow progress. A magpie jay wearing bold black, white and blue colors sat in the trees and cawed at me for a while. But then it was quiet. Everyone else must have been taking a siesta.

As I rounded a bend in the road I felt a wave of cool relief pass over me. There was a stream trickling down a gully lined with greenery where some farmers had left a grove of trees standing to protect their water supply. The grove felt like an oasis in the desert. The air was cool and fresh and there was plenty of entertaining wildlife.

I was in just the right condition for watching animals: too tired to move a muscle. I sat quietly, sipping at my water bottle, as bright yellowish-green and black butterflies rested on the leaves or danced above my head. Some of them, patterned in soft blues, were looping and diving in the air. As they chased one another they made rapid clicking noises. They were the only butterflies I have ever heard of that have a voice.

A squirrel with a silver and cinnamon coat came nervously down a tree trunk. It turned its hind feet backwards to grip the bark like hooks so that it could swing out head-first from the trunk, like a trapeze artist. It was a neat trick for reaching the tempting seedy tops of the tall grasses growing by the tree.

I was really starting to enjoy my refreshing and entertaining rest when I heard a low, rumbling noise coming along the road. It was the bus to the mountains. I quickly clambered up to the dusty roadside, waving wildly, and the bus screeched to a halt to pick me up. In the tropics few rural people can afford cars, so countless battered buses crawl through the countryside, crammed full of people, supplies and chickens.

I squeezed and shoved my way into an aisle already packed with people belly to belly. There was no politeness about finding a space. Squash yourself into it and it's yours.

The bus lunged into gear with a horrible grinding noise, and off we went. It was a wild ride. Music blared from loudspeakers in the bus, babies bawled, chickens clucked and the bus engine groaned and moaned as it tackled the steep hills. Sometimes the bus stopped to inch its way across dry creek beds of large rocks before lurching like a roller-coaster around a downhill curve. The road seemed to be following a trail laid out not by engineers and surveyors, but by a wild tapir, one of the huge grazing mammals that used to roam this area when there was forest here.

To add to the atmosphere of sweat and dust, someone had vomited. I kept mumbling the Spanish expression "Que será será," which means "Whatever will be will be." It reminded me to relax, since complaining would not get us to the end of the road any faster.

Going faster would probably not have been a good idea in any case. The road up the mountain was narrow with sharp turns. In stretches it was carved into the face of a steep slope with nothing but a sheer drop on the other side. We passed by a place where a battered yellow bus had gone over the edge and rolled over and over down into a gully.

It was late afternoon before I saw our destination up ahead. A green mountain ridge loomed above us: Monteverde. As we went higher, the landscape became green and lush. In the mountains there is plenty of moisture, even when it is dry season down below. I could look back down over the foothills and the mountainous spine of a large peninsula jutting out into the shining Pacific Ocean. The sun hovered above the horizon like a huge red molten ball and its low yellowing light turned the foothills to gold.

It was dark when I got off the bus. I headed uphill toward the collection of farms and homes known as Monteverde. Monteverde means "green mountain" in Spanish. It was a hopeful name and the night air had a hopeful feeling too. A cool wind washed over me, carrying mountain mist and the fresh smell of green trees.

A Forest in the Clouds

The next morning I awoke feeling confused. Where was I? I stuck my head out of my sleeping bag and peered around. There was a stalk of green bananas hanging from the ceiling rafter above my bed. The walls of the room were rough hand-sawn boards. A turquoise-crowned bird of a kind I had never seen before was sitting just outside the open window, singing a song I had never heard before — "mot-mot, mot-mot." Beyond the house was a green panorama of pasture and patches of forest. It took a few seconds to remember I was in a rented cabin on a mountain in Costa Rica.

As I looked out of the window I realized how good it would be to have a solid roof and shelter here. It was not ideal weather for camping with cameras, notebooks and field equipment. A cloud that was half mist and half rain was gusting and periodically shaking the trees and the roof. This part of the rain forest is high enough to be getting its moisture right from such clouds, so it is called cloud forest.

I was ready for a hot meal. I found a frying pan and sliced some of the bananas lengthwise. They were big cooking bananas; fried with a little sugar and cinnamon they made a sturdy breakfast that would keep me going all day.

As soon as the cloud lifted I set off uphill on the road to the Monteverde Cloud Forest Reserve. After half an hour of hiking past dairy farms I was at the edge of the protected jungle, an area where hunting and tree-cutting are forbidden.

As soon as I headed off the road into the thick forest, I knew I had stepped into a new world. As my eyes adjusted to the dim light I was surprised to see ferns the size of trees rising like feathery umbrellas high above my head. Vines hung like heavy ropes twisting down from the treetops. I couldn't resist grabbing one string dangling from the top of a mighty fig tree. To my surprise it was extremely elastic and strong. Although it was no thicker than a chubby pencil, it held firm as I swung out over a gully and back again. It was like riding a giant rubber band.

The jungle was the greenest place I'd ever seen. There were more shades of green in this forest than anyone could ever name. One reason it seemed so green was that every tree seemed to support its own little world of other plants. There were plants piled on top of other plants. On the tree trunks and branches mosses, orchids and even other small trees were growing.

It was a dark, damp place. But sometimes a shaft of sunlight would break through from above, shining through the gloom like the beam of a searchlight. Here and there along the trail, orchids, bromeliads and other plants were flowering, splashing a bright spray of color against the greenery. And as I walked quietly a brilliant blue or emerald hummingbird would flash by me and then stop to hover, using its long bill to drink nectar from the flowers.

I climbed up on a branch to look at a special kind of pineapple plant, a tank bromeliad, a huge clump of spiky leaves. They were all joined at the base so that they would catch and hold rainwater. As I looked down into the bromeliad's base I saw that it was like a miniature pond, complete with wiggling mosquito larvae, snails and even tadpoles. The plant debris was decaying and dissolving, the animals were growing, digesting, excreting, living and dying. The result was a nutritious soup that fed the bromeliad. So by providing living space for a small watery world of other creatures, the bromeliad had solved the problem of living out of touch with the earth below.

There are even some bromeliads that have their own digestive glands and chemicals. That gives them the ability to eat meat. And I had heard that at the very top of the mountain there were other kinds of meat-eating plants that capture and digest small insects, mites and other animals. Off I went, hoping to see them and another very unusual

creature, the rare golden toad.

The trail toward the mountaintop cut sideways up through a really steep section of extremely lush cloud forest that was incredibly soggy. As I squelched along in my rubber boots, the top of the mountain appeared suddenly. One minute I was enclosed in tall heavy forest, and the next minute I stepped out into an open area surrounded by trees barely higher than my head. Looking west I could see the shining surface of the Pacific Ocean, and in the east I could see the dark green of the Atlantic lowlands. Standing up there I could feel the full strength of the trade winds that blow from the Atlantic. They were flapping my clothes, and I had to lean into the wind when I walked.

Above: Bromeliad in flower
Left: Green-crowned hummingbird pollinating a flower

The force of these moisture-laden winds had smoothly shaped the woodlands into a green blanket hugging the Atlantic face of the mountain. From the mountaintop, it looked just as though it had been neatly raked with a giant comb.

But inside, the forest on the Atlantic side was anything but neat. The trees were gnarled and bent every which way. It was impossible to tell where one tree ended and another began because everything was draped in soggy masses of moss. The ground was a tangle of roots and fallen branches. When the clouds began drifting through the twisted, almost lifelike shapes, I understood why botanists call this "elfin forest." It was an eerie place to be.

This patch of elfin cloud forest is the only place on Earth where one can find golden toads. It was getting dark when I found the first puddle surrounded by toads. Not all the toads were golden. Only the males were a brilliant orange-gold all over; the females were brown and mottled with red and black markings. When a female plunged into a pool she was mobbed by the crowd of males. The males wrestled and rolled into a giant golden ball wrapped around the female. Each male was trying to be the one to fertilize the female's eggs. The female released her masses of eggs into the puddle and they immediately swelled into the typical frog egg shape, clear balls with tiny dark embryonic tadpoles in the center. Soon the pool was a squirming jelly soup of eggs and toads.

A golden toad releases her eggs under water.

I had come a long way in one day, and it was time to think about finding a place to spend the night. I continued along the ridge and down to a shack maintained as a shelter by the Cloud Forest Reserve. Supper was crackers and canned tuna, which tasted unexpectedly delicious. Hunger is the best sauce, they say.

I slipped into my sleeping bag. For a few minutes I lay awake listening to the wind rattle the tin roofing. I could hear forest mice scuttling up and down the walls hunting for insects. But soon I fell into a heavy and sound sleep.

The next morning I decided to get off the trail and follow a riverbed back down to Monteverde. I knew the river passed right below my cabin. It was a rough route back. The riverbed was a jumble of slick round boulders, waterfalls and fallen trees. Once, as I jumped from a rock to a log, the rotten wood gave way and I pitched face first into the water.

When I reached the stretch of river just below my cabin, I took a breather under a towering twisted tree standing weirdly on a row of great legs. It was a giant strangler fig, the largest tree in the forest.

A strangler starts life as a tiny seed that a fig-eating parrot or monkey drops in the top of a tree. The seed lodges in the crease where a limb joins the trunk. Rotten leaves collect there, and the seedling begins to grow in the mulch. As soon as it has turned into a small bush, the strangler begins to dangle long roots down to the ground. It was on one of these aerial roots that I had been swinging earlier. When the roots touch the earth they grow rapidly, anchoring and feeding the strangler tree high at the top of the host tree. The fig now puts on a spurt of growth. It shoots up, growing higher than the host on which it is growing, and puts out a dense umbrella of leaves. As the host tree grows weaker, starving in the shade, the fig grows stronger. Its dangling roots become woody, and as they touch one another they fuse together, wrapping the host tree inside a solid curtain of fig. Shaded and perhaps squeezed, the host tree eventually dies, giving up its space in the forest to the strangler fig.

I saw that the roots of this strangler had grown and fused, but not completely. There were cracks and crannies everywhere. These protected spaces had become homes for many animals. Using a pencil I poked around in one of these holes. I jumped back when a big mother scorpion came scuttling out with her stinger tail held up in the air.

Right:
The giant legs of a strangler fig
Far Right:
Dangling roots of a strangler surround a host tree.

I knew it was a mother because her back was covered with baby scorpions. The mother scorpion carries her young around so that she can keep them out of harm's reach. She is better at catching food than her youngsters, so they stay with her until they are large enough to catch supper by themselves. Until then the mother grabs large insects such as cockroaches with her strong pincers, then prepares a meal by chewing open the skin of the roach and adding her saliva, which is full of digestive enzymes. These enzymes begin to pre-digest the food. The young scorpions can then climb down and drink their dinner of liquid cockroach.

I wondered what was living in the space left when the dead tree rotted away. When I stuck my head inside, the hollow rang with high-pitched squeaks. Mice? I shone my flashlight up. Squeaking bats were hanging upside down with their wings wrapped around their bodies like cloaks. At night

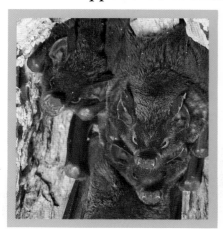

the bats would fly out and catch insects such as moths. It seemed that insects were sometimes brought back to the bat roost, because I saw moth wings piled beneath the tree. Ants were busily scavenging, cleaning up these crumbs beneath the bats' dining area and carrying them down into their nests under the forest floor.

24

The fig had killed another tree and I could see that now it was being eaten, in its turn, by caterpillars. These caterpillars would turn into moths. The fig also provided a haven for bats. The bats caught the moths and left food for the ants. The ants loosened the earth, and when they died their bodies would enrich the soil. Finally, the roots of the fig and other trees would absorb the nutrients in the soil.

Each animal and plant was working, providing something useful for some other organism. When a plant or animal died, its body was quickly converted into a new form of life. All around the strangler fig this recycling was going on right before my eyes.

There is something about a huge old tree that makes you stop and wonder about the meaning of things. I sat on a rock in the river. Alone in the forest I found peace and quiet and the time to think. What did that name ''killer tree'' mean? Is a strangler fig good, or is it bad because it lives by killing other trees? All the life around the fig made the answer clear to me. The death of one tree had meant life for other creatures. Because everything is connected in the forest, life and death are never wasted.

High Life

"Aaaaarrrrrooooooo — oooo — oooo — gaaaahhhh!" I almost jumped out of my rubber boots. It sounded as if there was a huge and fierce creature right above me. Branches were rattling, sticks and leaves rained down, along with an avalanche of noise.

I had startled a large male howler monkey feeding at the end of a branch not far above my head. And he had startled *me*! The howler glared down, shaking the shaggy mane and beard around his face. He thrust out his strong lower jaw and began bellowing out more threats at me.

I wasn't worried. Howlers are big monkeys, but they are harmless in spite of their fearsome calls. In fact the animal's annoyance was my good luck. I had hoped to get a good look at the special equipment the male howler has for producing his deep roars.

I could see clearly that his throat was massive, with a giant voice box. He was using this sound system for producing deep gravelly bass notes.

The howler's roaring is an important social behavior directed at other howler monkeys. A troop normally roars together, led by the largest dominant male. These howling sessions begin each morning as the monkeys wake up. Often they repeat the chorus just before bedding down in the treetops for the night. You can hear the calls echoing down the vast valleys. The clamor advertises their location and probably discourages other troops from using the same area of forest and fighting over the same feeding trees.

Soon I came upon the rest of the howler troop, quietly feeding on leaf buds. Small babies were riding on their mothers' backs or clinging to their bellies as the females wandered slowly from one branch to another, looking for fresh new growth. They seemed slow and sleepy. Sometimes they would stop feeding to scratch, groom each other or do a little sunbathing, dozing peacefully with their legs draped over the tree limbs. One of their common gestures was to stick their tongues out at one another. It was just like watching a family on a picnic.

I was glad I had my binoculars because most of the monkeys were high above my head. It was the binoculars that helped me spot an animal so slow it made the howler monkeys look like racecars.

Grasping tightly onto a branch by a set of long arms and legs with huge claws was a two-toed sloth. It was a female, carrying her baby. They remained completely motionless, and their coats of long greenish-gray hair kept them well camouflaged. Because tiny green algae grow all through their hair, sloths at rest look like big chunks of moss.

The reason why the English name for this animal is "sloth" and its Spanish name means "lazy" is that it moves slowly to save energy. The sloth uses energy at half the rate of other mammals its size. Its body temperature is also lower than that of most mammals, which helps the sloth get by on its low-energy diet of leaves. At night the body temperature of a sloth may drop close to the air temperature, and it becomes even more sluggish. It's as though the sloth goes into hibernation every time the sun goes down. When the sun comes up in the morning, a sloth often heads for a basking spot on an exposed limb where it sprawls out just like a lizard, letting the sun's energy gently bring its body temperature up again. After a sunbath, the sloth is ready for a new day.

Sloth mother and infant spend their days eating leaves and sleeping.

On this hike I hadn't set out with anything particular in mind. I had just started heading downhill into the forest, hoping to get more sunshine. But it was turning out to be a great day. Seeing monkeys and sloths was what this trip was all about.

As I worked my way along a sharp cliff edge, I saw what I thought was a very familiar animal, a porcupine. It had been eating flat velvety-brown seed pods in an inga tree. The porcupine didn't seem interested in running away, and I got a good look at it. It was smaller than our North American porcupine and less spiny, and its tail was naked, like a giant rat tail. The North American porcupine has a club-like tail covered with a bristling coat of spines. But this porcupine's tail is more like the tail of a monkey or possum. It can be used as another holding limb, a clear sign that the porcupine is well equipped for life in the treetops.

By hoisting myself a short way up the trunk, I found the cavity the porcupine used as a retreat. I could probably have found it just by using my nose — it was giving off a powerful stench. Like many of the mammals who live spread out in the treetops, porcupines communicate their presence and position by marking the trees with urine or other smelly glandular secretions.

The cliff edge looked like a good place for a rest and a water stop. I stretched out in the sun and watched the vultures gliding overhead. They spiraled round and round in huge circuits. Riding on the hot air currents, they never had to move a muscle. I felt just as relaxed and was on the verge of a siesta when I heard a thrashing and whooping on the slope below. I suspected the commotion was being caused by spider monkeys.

I jumped up and began working my way down through the trees along the steep slope, trying to get a glimpse of these agile skinny monkeys. They are called spider monkeys because of their long skinny limbs and tails. Their hands and feet are also long so that their fingers can wrap firmly around branches. The agile tail can grab at branches, just like an arm, and it is strong enough to allow the tiny monkey to dangle without any other support. These features enable spider monkeys to swing wildly arm over arm at high speed through the treetops. They seem to be fearless leapers, running down

30

to the end of a branch and springing out into space with their arms spread, then landing in the next tree crown. They are exciting and uncommon, and I was eager to get a good look at them.

It was almost my last look at anything! I was trying so hard to get a better look at the monkeys that I found myself slipping in a slurry of loose earth and dry leaves down a steep slope. At the bottom of the slope was a bone-breaking drop. It was sheer luck that I grabbed a mass of dangling tree roots and stopped my slide before I reached the edge. Slowly I pulled myself hand over hand to the base of a large tree, then up to the next tree, until I was on secure footing.

That was enough monkey-watching for the day. Or so I thought.

Later that afternoon I was back sitting in the loft of my cabin, writing up my field notes, when I got the funny feeling that someone was watching me. I looked out the window. In the trees beside the house was a troop of white-faced monkeys; *they* were doing the watching this time. They stared at me seriously with

Left: *White-faced monkeys are among the most intelligent of all monkeys.* Right: *Howler mother and baby*

the most intelligent faces for a few seconds, and then continued on their travels.

31

Wings of the Jungle

One of the things I was enjoying most about being in Costa Rica was all the tropical fruits I could buy. There were orange-fleshed papayas, tangy star fruits, rich red sapotes, slippery white lichees, juicy golden mangoes, creamy custard apples and rich oily avocadoes for sale.

All these fruits, now cultivated in many parts of the world, were first discovered growing wild in jungles. So I knew I could find wild fruits in the Monteverde jungle, and I planned to look for the birds that feed upon them on my next hike.

It didn't take long for me to find fruit-eating birds. As I stepped out of a woodlot and into a sheltered pasture, a pair of the gaudiest birds I had ever seen flew by me. Their ruby-red chests and streaming long emerald tails flashed brilliantly

as they climbed steeply up into the air and plunged down across the clearing. I had stumbled on quetzals (pronounced *ket-sals*), some of the most beautiful birds in the world.

The quetzals were feeding mostly on a kind of wild avocado, a fat glossy black fruit that looked like a giant olive. A quetzal would fly to the tip of an avocado branch to pluck a fruit off. Then it would fly off to another tree to perch with the avocado held in its bill. It opens its mouth fantastically wide and almost magically swallows the avocado whole. A short while later it spits out the large hard seed, but without its coat of oily black flesh.

I picked up some of the avocado seeds. They were big and as hard as cherry pits — too large and solid for the quetzal to pass through its digestive system. Like most fruit-eating birds the quetzal has a soft stomach. When it eats, it removes the fleshy coating around the pit and then coughs the seed up and out. Under one perch where I had seen quetzals eating avocadoes were hundreds of seeds; some had even sprouted.

This made it clear to me why fleshy rich fruits developed in the tropical forest. Their bright tasty flesh feeds the birds, and the birds disperse the seeds to places where the young tree seedlings can get started.

As I walked on through the forest, I began to take more notice of the colors and arrangements of the fruits. In the midst of all the greenery, the clusters of bright orange, bold red and black, and pink and yellow berries and fruits were really eye-catching. I tried sampling some, but few of them were sweet enough for my taste.

I found a fig tree along the road that was loaded with emerald toucanets. There were at least six of these birds feeding so busily that I was sure the little pink figs must be delicious. They were using their long colorful bills like tweezers to pluck the pink figs, toss them back in the air and swallow, all with one quick flick of the head.

As I watched, a larger keel-billed toucan flew in and all the toucanets scattered. The

toucan was even more fantastically colored. But it was a bit nervous at my presence and soon left, giving me an opportunity to try the figs myself. To my disappointment they tasted totally bland. Evidently the birds could appreciate something that I couldn't.

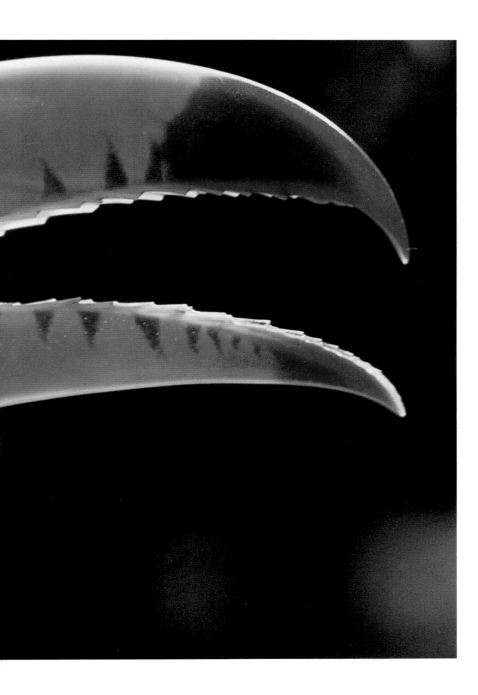

In fact, along the same stretch of road I saw brilliant yellow, green and blue chlorophonias eating mistletoe berries. I knew that mistletoe berries are poisonous for people. But the chlorophonias are able to digest the fruit covering without damaging or digesting any of the poisonous seeds. As a result the mistletoe has its seeds spread all through the jungle by the chlorophonias.

This relationship is good for the mistletoe but bad for the trees. When a bird deposits a mistletoe seed on a tree branch, the seed sprouts and its roots burrow into the tree. The mistletoe roots then absorb water and nutrients from the tree's circulatory system. It was clear that the chlorophonias were doing an effective job of seed dispersal because there was mistletoe all over the trees. But evidently the relationship was a tolerable one because the trees were green and healthy-looking in spite of their unwanted guests.

Heading back across a pasture near my cabin, I watched a bird damaging a tree more directly. A red-headed woodpecker was pounding a nest hole in the side of the tree. Each chiseling stroke of the head made a powerful thunk as the bill dug in. To me it seemed incredible that a bird could pound away like that without damaging its brain or at least getting a severe headache. Nearby were a pair of masked tityras, delightful white birds with black face masks and metallic twangy voices, watching the woodpecker at work.

Tityras can't make their own nest holes, so they often steal those of woodpeckers or even those of large birds like toucans. The big woodpeckers and toucans are strong enough to throw the tityras out, so the tityras don't confront them directly; they just pester the bigger birds into leaving. Every time the owners go away to forage, the tityras bring leaves and trash and stuff them in the nest hole. When they return the owners remove it, but the tityras keep stuffing it back in. Eventually the bigger birds give up and the tityras take over the space.

It was late in the day and the woodpecker was still working while the tityras were just watching. So I headed on, hoping to watch this relationship develop on another day.

Right: *Pale-billed woodpecker hammers out a nest.* Far Right: *Quetzal habitat in Monteverde*

Afraid of the Dark

In Monteverde the sun was my alarm clock. Sunrise set off a chorus of bird songs that made sleeping impossible. It seemed like the liveliest time in the rain forest. But I knew that many of the animals in the jungle actually wake up at sunset and are most active during the night. To really see the wildlife, I would have to visit the forest after sundown. The thought of hiking through the jungle in the dark made me both excited and nervous.

Late one afternoon I packed my headlamp, some spare batteries, my camera and flash, and a chunk of cheese and set off uphill. When I reached the edge of the woods the sun was already sinking toward the golden foothills and the Pacific Ocean. As it slipped below the horizon,

I made my way into the forest. A fallen log made a convenient bench and I took a seat, waiting for night to fall. It was like sitting in a deep hole. The clouds above still glowed, but the jungle interior was dissolving into a misty gloom.

Soon streaks and spots of cool green light began to pulse in the dark. I knew they were the courting signals of the fireflies and click beetles. But knowing that did not make the flickering lights and the black shapes of trees in the heavy shadows any less eerie.

I was amazed to see that the end of my log was also glowing with a strange green light. But this light did not go out. I bent my head forward and pushed my face right up to the pale shape: mushrooms. I could smell and feel them. Flickering fireflies were familiar, but I couldn't guess why mushrooms would shine in the dark, and so their soft glow added more mystery to the dark.

The forest was also filling up with all kinds of strange sounds. Whistles, whoops and chirpings were coming from every direction. Without the use of my eyes, my ears seemed much more sensitive. I could hear the swooping bats above me and the whining mosquito circling my head.

There were rustling noises in the leaves beside me. My nose was picking up the heavy perfume of flowers and the earthy scent of decaying leaves. I felt surrounded by invisible activity and sensations.

I wanted to wait as long as possible in the dark, soaking up the sounds, the smells, the feeling of night in the jungle. Then something ran across my hand. I jumped up electrified. It was time to turn on the lights.

I felt for my headlamp and switched on the light. As soon as I looked around, I realized this had been a sensible decision. Right beside me was a large scorpion armed with a long, powerful stinging tail. That was one nighttime sensation I did not want to experience. The scorpion was munching on a katydid, so I left it to enjoy its breakfast without my company.

Walking along the trail with my headlamp lighting the way was like walking slowly through a long dark tunnel. The forest all around me was inky black, and all my attention was focused on the narrow circle of light just ahead of me. My eyes were watching the ground right ahead of my feet. When I wanted to look up, I had to stop and stand still to avoid crashing into trees. I found this slow-moving and concentrated viewpoint was a great way of discovering small animals I might miss during the day, when sunlight exposed the whole forest all at once.

I saw slippery-looking salamanders in the leaves, waiting to capture insects. In the middle of a raspberry patch my light surprised a tiny harvest mouse not much bigger than the raspberries he was eating. He had long whiskers to detect objects around his face and huge dark eyes for night vision.

The vegetation was crawling with long-legged tree frogs whose fingers and toes ended in broad flat suckers, which let them cling to the leaves. Their huge bulging eyes helped them see under dim light. I envied the mouse and the frogs their large eyes. If I turned off my headlamp I would see absolutely nothing. I was totally dependent on my batteries and the fragile filament in the light bulb. Looking for large eyes turned out to be the easiest way to find mammals. I stood still and slowly swept my headlamp through the treetops until a pair of burning red lights shone toward me from a tree. When I walked closer, I could see the lights were porcupine eyes. They were reflecting the light of my headlamp back at me.

Porcupines, like most night-active mammals, have a shiny layer on the back inner surface of their eyes that helps to gather light and reflect it.

To my surprise I saw tiny eyes shining like clusters of rubies on the forest floor. When I got down on my hands and knees I discovered they were the eyes of small spiders. At least, some of them were small. I found myself sharing one section of the trail with a large hairy black and pinkish tarantula the size of a  saucer. It was a female dragging her white sac full of eggs. After my initial surprise I found it was fascinating to watch the tarantula moving placidly along with her many-jointed legs all moving rhythmically up and down. It was a good reason for me to walk carefully.

Not all the animals I saw were awake. I  noticed many sleeping lizards on the ferns and palm fronds beside the trail. They didn't seem to mind my light at all. The curious thing about the lizards was that they were always out on the very tips of the long dangling fronds.

I wondered if the lizards were positioning themselves there at the very tips of the leaves as a kind of early warning system to detect approaching snakes, possums and other animals that eat lizards. When the predator approaches, it can't avoid bumping into the delicate fern or palm frond, and the tremor alerts the lizard. I tried out my theory by gently jiggling a fern where a lizard was sleeping. It worked! The lizard let go and scuttled off as soon as it hit the ground.

Unfortunately for the lizards there is one snake, the chunk-headed snake, that is able to get around the warning system. It has special sections in its backbone that can lock together and allow the snake to extend its body almost half its length without any other support. This enables the snake to reach far out into empty space. When the snake locates a sleeping lizard, it can approach it from a neighboring plant. Without disturbing the lizard's plant, the snake can reach across and grab the unsuspecting prey.

Left: Anole lizard shedding its skin Right: *Chunk-headed snake (also seen far left) captures a sleeping lizard.*

I was starting to relax a little as I got used to the nightlife. But as I passed under a steep bank, my calm was interrupted by a sudden crunching, tearing sound. I stopped in my tracks and looked up. A furry brown animal with a long dangling tail was biting into the stem of a tree fern. It was a kinkajoo ripping out the soft pithy insides of the stem and swallowing large mouthfuls.

The kinkajoo turned toward me and was momentarily blinded by my headlamp. He couldn't see me but he could smell me, and the smell was making him nervous. He hopped toward me and perched on a vine. Snuffing and snorting, he leaned down so close that I could almost touch his furry head. I knew this would be a mistake. I

could see his strong claws and powerful jaws, and he looked like a feisty animal who would defend himself. So I quickly snapped off my light. The kinkajoo leaped by and went crashing away through the undergrowth.

The face-to-face encounter with such a strong personality had set my pulse racing. Without realizing it, I had been holding my breath the entire time. I found myself another log to sit on and kept my light turned off for a while.

As my heartbeat slowed, I again became more aware of the exotic sounds and scents of the jungle. There were calls from animals that I still hadn't found, heady scents from flowers high above that I couldn't see. But I had already seen so many unfamiliar animals that it seemed like I had been exploring a new world for most of the night.

I checked my watch and was startled to see that it was only eight o'clock. There was plenty of night left to enjoy. But I decided to enjoy it in a quieter, more familiar place. I took out my piece of cheese and, chewing it hungrily, headed carefully home through the mysterious velvet darkness to my supper and bed.

Flashers and Fakers

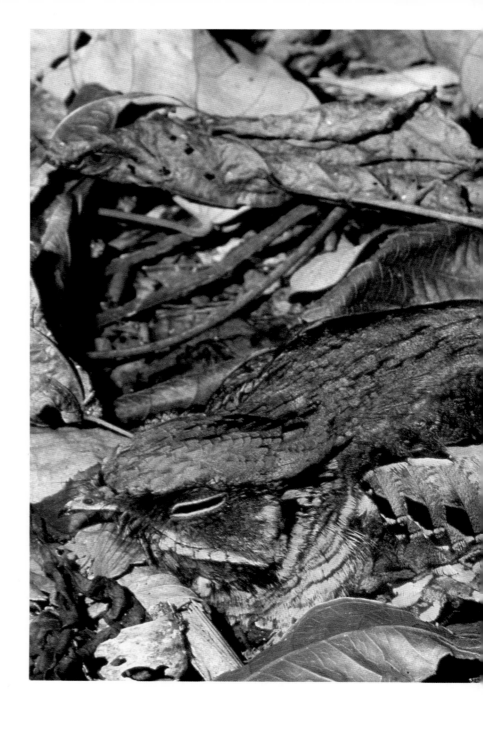

One of my goals on this trip was to collect flies for a friend of mine, a scientist who was studying a special kind of fly. These flies are fast, and the only way I could catch them was to walk slowly along the trails and net the flies when they were sunning themselves on leaves. This calm, quiet way of walking helped me discover some of the cleverly camouflaged animals of the jungle.

One morning on my favorite fly-catching route, a path that ran down through the forest to a coffee farm, I spotted a large boa constrictor on the ground. The wavy pattern of the boa's skin made it blend in with the leaves, helping the boa to catch a mouse or some other small mammal that

was moving too fast and too carelessly to notice it.

Lower down in the valley I almost stepped on an even better mimic of dead leaves. A long winged bird fluttered up from under my foot.

It was a pauraqué (pronounced *par-ah-kay*), a kind of whippoorwill that nests on the ground during the day and hunts insects by night. Any bird that nests on the ground has to be very skilled at hiding from its enemies. I had seen for myself how difficult it is to spot one of these birds sitting still.

One day I was walking along, looking for flies, when I suddenly stopped and jumped back without really knowing why. I looked down, and at my feet was an unusually beautiful snake. Its markings were bold and bright, the exact opposite of camouflage. When I realized the snake was banded with shiny rings of black and red, I jumped back even farther. I was glad I was wearing my tall rubber boots. It was a dazzling but deadly coral snake, with venom strong enough to paralyze and kill a human.

But the snake had no interest in harming me. Snakes, after all, have no arms or legs to help them capture food, so this coral snake couldn't have been considering anything as big as me for dinner. Their venom is simply a special saliva used to subdue more suitable prey and then help digest it. But they also use their poisonous bite to defend themselves from animals that step on them. So the bright colors of the coral had done us both a favor. They provided a warning that had stopped me from injuring the snake, and my retreat had stopped the snake from having to bite me in self-defence.

I got another jolt when I was inspecting a shrub covered with little berries. I jerked away in fear when a small green snake reared up.

When I looked closer I realized that the snake was actually a caterpillar. It had fake eyespots on its body, and the muscles along its side were contracted to create the impression of a thin neck and a swollen snake head. The caterpillar's real head and eyes were tiny and located right at its very tip. But by rearing up and waving back and forth, it had frightened me off at first. It was easy to see that it might have the same effect on a lizard or frog.

I reached into the bush and grabbed the caterpillar. In my hand it looked completely harmless, and it was. Looking at it I wondered how this squirming worm-like creature could have fooled me. But when snakes are involved, we jump first and think about it later.

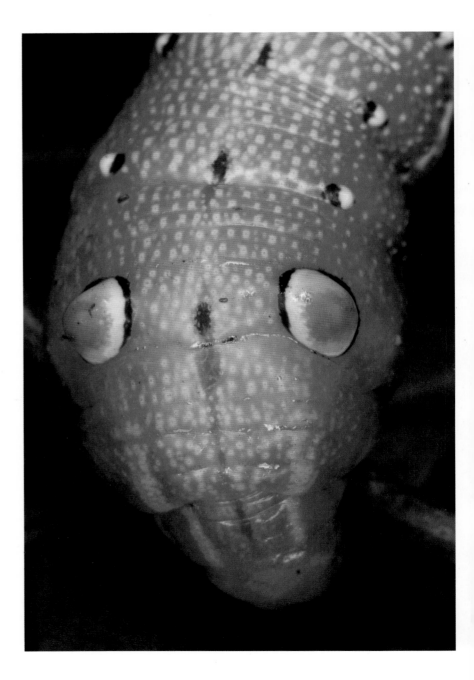

Finding the false snake caterpillar got me interested in caterpillars, and I spent more time looking for them on my walks around Monteverde. The most amazing group I found was a mass of large yellow and pink Io caterpillars. They were as long as my hand and covered with long delicate spines that looked like glass crystals. Dozens of these caterpillars were all over a shrub, chewing its leaves. As I walked around the shrub, I accidentally brushed my bare arm against them. Immediately my skin began to burn red hot, and a huge red welt sprang up, as though I had just been whipped. The delicate-looking spines had embedded themselves in my skin. The painful burning lasted for hours, and my arm continued to itch for several days. It was an unforgettable learning experience: I had learned never to bother these caterpillars.

One of the best places I found to observe insects was right on the front porch of my cabin. I left some bright lights burning out there every night, and they attracted hundreds of night-flying insects like moths and beetles. When morning came and the air was cool, hundreds or even thou-sands of moths and other insects would be sitting quietly all over the porch and I could inspect them at my leisure. It was on my porch that I found other kinds of insects that use false eyes in a startling way.

Some of the largest insects I saw were adult Io moths, the grown-up version of the caterpillar I had brushed against. They sat completely still with their drab forewings folded down, like cloaks over their bodies and hind wings. It was hard to tell if they were dead or alive. But when I poked one of these moths it seemed to explode. The forewings flashed ahead and two big fierce eyeballs glared out at me. I drew back instinctively.

The moth had just performed a startling illusion. The eyes were created by the colored scales on the hind wings. The eyeballs looked real, as though they had been painted by a skilled artist. It was exactly what I remembered being told about painting eyes in art class. The eyeball was created by a dense black circle, surrounded by a lighter area. In the center a sprinkling of white scales created the effect of light reflecting off the eye.

There was a good reason for this fine artwork. I saw real eyes just like this when I noticed two spectacled owls in a tree. Small birds are frightened of owls because many owls eat small birds. By flashing their hind wings into view, imitating the face of an owl, the moths frighten

away the birds and keep themselves from being eaten. The moth had reacted to my poking as though I was a pecking bird. And in my surprise I had reacted a bit like a bird.

There was even more amazing artwork around my porch. There were moths that looked just like dead sticks and old leaves. Their wings were gray and brown, with fine lines and spots looking like tree bark or leaf veins, and they were twisted in crinkled, wrinkled shapes. They even had blotchy patches on them that looked like mold and fungus. I found that these moths did not react at all like the Io moths when I poked them. The moths that looked like dead twigs stayed com-

pletely still, and the ones that looked like dead leaves let go of the branches they were resting on and fluttered slowly to the ground.

I gently carried some over to a tree trunk near the cabin and let them settle on the surface. When some friends came by later in the day, I led them over to the tree trunk to see if they could spot anything there. They were mystified. It was only when I pointed them out that they could see the moths. Looking very carefully we could see that these twigs and leaves had legs.

While we were looking at the moths, we noticed some moss that was moving. How could that be? I took a closer look. We had discovered a moss katydid. Its head, legs and body were coated with long spines that mimicked the color and texture of the mossy lichen. It was eating the pale green lichen and looked like a living version of the expression "You are what you eat."

Not all the displays of insects were camouflaged. Near my porch light I found bright blue and pink moths. These reacted to my prodding in their own distinctive way. They began blowing bubbles of yellowish foam out of openings on their bodies just behind their heads. In only a second each moth had built a frothy mess half as large as itself. I suspected this foam was some obnoxious chemical mixture that would discourage birds and monkeys from eating the moths.

Dipping my fingertip into the foam, I tasted just the tiniest bit. Yuck! I was right. It was so bitter I had to run inside the cabin and rinse my mouth out over and over again to get rid of the taste. Those moths looked better than they tasted.

Each day I was learning more about animal signals.
And each day I marveled at the result of these signals: a forest full of beautiful designs and colors.

Left: *Moss katydid*
Right: *Moths camouflaged on tree bark*
Far Right: *Moth excretes a bright repellent foam* .

Getting Wilder

My alarm began beeping while it was still dark. First I stumbled into the kitchen to start heating water for coffee; then I began to stuff my backpack. I wrapped my sleeping bag, binoculars and camera gear inside plastic garbage bags. Along with an umbrella, the bags would be essential protection for a hike down into one of the wettest valleys in Costa Rica.

This was going to be a very tough trek, with rivers, streams and mudslides along the way, so I pulled on my trusty rubber boots. I packed plenty of dried bananas, caramels and other lightweight foods that would give me lots of energy on the steep muddy trail. Several spare pairs of socks would be useful, as well as candles and extra batteries for the flashlight: there would be no electricity down there. A mosquito net of fine mesh was vital for sleeping in an area with tiny biting flies. Insect-collecting gear and a machete for odd jobs took up the rest of the room in the pack. I gulped down a large glass of coffee and milk, hoisted my pack and began trudging up the moonlit road.

Along the road I met a couple of other biologists working in Monteverde who would be my company for the hike. We had to head uphill first on our way to the valley, and our progress was slow. Dawn at the top of the cloud forest brought with it heavy clouds of blowing mist. It was too windy for umbrellas and too warm for rain ponchos, so we were soon damp. But all the exercise meant we were hot in spite of being wet. We were blowing off steam and sweating like workhorses when we took our first rest stop at a lookout over the Peñas Blancas River valley, a place with no roads, cars or towns, just ridge after ridge of unbroken jungle stretching as far as the eye could see.

The route ahead of us was suitable only for human feet and horse's hooves. Parts of the track were a running river of water. Other sections were cobbled by broken stone, which suddenly changed to a boggy quagmire of greasy clay and mud. It took a mixture of plodding, jumping, wading and slithering to travel this route.

After about half an hour of steady downhill slogging, the trail narrowed. We took another break to refill our water bottles in a clear stream and to look around at the changing scenery.

Already it felt much hotter and there were many new trees to observe. Palm trees rose up as straight and slim as arrows tipped with a bunch of fronds. A huge hibiscus covered with purple trumpet flowers the size of my opened hand cast its shadow over us. Swallow-tailed kites, large forktailed birds that eat flying insects and sail and soar like the most graceful kites, were landing in the tops of huge trees, looking for places to build nests. These new sights were a welcome diversion because I was rediscovering the pain that is part of backpacking.

Muscles I hadn't used in a long time rebelled against the strain of carrying a heavy load up and down hills. My lungs and heart weren't

used to supplying the huge quantities of oxygen that my muscles were burning. I knew that sitting and resting often was no solution. My muscles would seize up and cramp if I sat. The best strategy seemed to be a slow steady pace and keeping my mind on the scenery rather than on how I was feeling.

As we worked our way along one of the rare flat stretches hugging a slope, I could hear a deep roar. Looking down a steep drop, I got my first glimpse of the Peñas Blancas River rolling and boiling white over its bed of boulders and river rock. It would be nice, I thought, if we could descend as easily as that rushing water on its journey to the Atlantic Ocean.

As we rounded a bend we startled several furry gray pig-like animals that were rooting alongside the trail. They saw us just as we saw them. One of them gnashed its large yellowish teeth at us. Then with a snort they whirled and crashed away into the forest. When they were gone I could still smell their strong gamey odor lingering along the trail.

They had good reason to hurry off. Peccaries are close relatives of the pigs we eat, and humans, jaguars and mountain lions often hunt and eat them. It was good to see peccaries here: it meant we were entering an area where people had not yet destroyed the wildlife.

In fact, we were now in a place where mountain lions hunted. A friend of mine had told me about a hike he had taken in this area. Hearing a squalling snarl nearby, he had looked up; above him a mountain lion was looking out from a bank of tangled vegetation, with his mouth spread wide, revealing tremendous dagger-like teeth. My friend had the nerve to snap a photograph, and then he and the great cat went in opposite directions.

The drizzle continued, and the trees got taller and taller as we descended lower and lower. I pulled my pant legs out of my boots because the water running down the pants kept filling the boots. My pants were getting heavy with a coat of greasy mud plastered well above my knees. I was glad every time we had to cross a small stream, because the current washed away the mud and lightened my load.

The next entertainment was a fresh land-slide. A section of the mountainside half the size of a football field had slipped loose, and a mass of

soaked mud and uprooted trees had slumped and slid down, burying the trail as it headed toward the river. The slide was so fresh that parts of it were still moving. We crossed around its base carefully, poking our way around the deepest soft spots and hoping it would not suddenly begin to flow again while we were in its path.

When we finally reached the edge of the Peñas Blancas River we saw our first sign of human habitation, a dilapidated house of rough hand-sawn boards, sagging with rot. It was obviously

abandoned and one could easily see why. The area was so wet that small streams were running around and under the house. Life there would be moldy and damp.

We began looking for a way to cross the river. Someone had attached a steel cable between two trees; hanging from it was a small wooden trolley that you could sit in to pull yourself across in the air. But the cable looked old. The water, on the other hand, seemed low enough to wade across, so we plunged in. It was not as easy as it

looked. The cold water surged up to our thighs and the river rocks were slick. With each step I struggled, balancing against the surge of the current on one leg while trying to place the other foot securely on a new rock. A slip would mean more than just a dunking. I could lose my backpack — or worse. But we all made it without a slip.

Our trail now ran along the edge of the river. We saw many new birds along the banks. There were tiny dippers that would dive into the churning rapids and fly along under water, searching for aquatic insects on the river bottom. But the

most spectacular of all the birds were the sun bitterns. Sitting still they looked like chubby versions of the heron. But when alarmed or when signaling other sun bitterns they spread their wings, revealing a huge pair of black and golden-orange eyespots.

An hour after we crossed the river, a howling hound dog announced our arrival at a working farm. Alejandro García's family looked out from the porch of their tiny cabin as we climbed up through the pasture. This was the first place where someone seemed to be surviving the

wetness of the valley. Two huge tom turkeys were fighting, puffing out their chests, fanning their tails and bumping each other in a battle for control of the farmyard. They looked healthy. But Alejandro's cows were skinny.

Alejandro's wife gave us the friendly welcome typical of Costa Rican people who live in the country. When they say "Our house is your house," they mean it. She brought us large jars of steaming hot sweet coffee and bowls of rice pudding. It was just the refueling we needed. Her bright-eyed children stood shyly staring at the first strangers they had seen in a long while.

Before we headed off downhill, we donated some boxes of cookies and canned tuna to Alejandro's household, and they were well received. There are no stores in this valley, and supplies are hard to come by. And there are no schools, no doctors, no telephones — none of the things we take for granted. As I walked away I wondered how Alejandro's children would ever get to school and how long the family could survive under such difficult conditions. Perhaps the Monteverde Reserve could buy their land and relocate the family in an area better suited to farming.

Our destination was another small farm that the reserve had just purchased. By midafternoon, the sun had burned through the clouds, so the air had grown hotter and steamier.

Finally we stood at the edge of the forest, looking down at another small tin-roofed cabin set up on stilts. This was the home of Eladio and Anise Cruz. Although the reserve had bought their farm to use as a base camp for biologists, Eladio's family had stayed on to run the camp, cut trails, bring in food and help with scientific research.

We crowded into the cabin and staked our claims for sleeping space on the floor. As we strung up our mosquito nets, Anise prepared supper. The air was filled with the smell of boiling beans and smoke from the cooking area, an open raised platform in one corner of the cabin. All the furniture, like the cabin itself, had been built by Eladio. It was like Eladio: lean, simple and solid. I could see why Eladio, who seemed like a shy person, also had a tremendous dignity. He lived an independent life based on hard work and self-reliance.

As it got dark, we lit candles and sat on benches crowded around a table. In spite of the language difficulties the talk was lively. With everyone sharing the same small living space — with no television, no books, no place to go for entertainment, in fact with hardly any distractions — the evening was right for good company and conversation.

And for eating! Anise began bringing in the food, the typical simple dishes that are served on small Costa Rican farms. There was a jug of water mixed with the tart refreshing juice from a sour orange tree, a pot of black beans, mounds of golden fried cooking bananas, sour cream made from the milk of one of Eladio's cows, and a plate of boiled elephant-ear roots.

The elephant-ear roots came from plants with huge leaves shaped like arrowheads. They are starchy, like potatoes, but with more protein and a rich nutty taste. Best of all, they grow locally with little care. No one has to lug them into the valley from someplace else. It was a bulky, high-calorie dinner, the kind of meal that brings on sleep quickly after a long day's hiking.

We rinsed our plates and retired to our places on the floor. When we snuffed the candles, rain began to drum on the tin roof and splatter in the muddy yard. As we bedded down, we could hear the farm animals doing the same. They had congregated under the house, out of the rain. I could hear the duck quacking and a few hens clucking below me. Once in a while a pig snorted or a calf bawled. Someone snored next to me and mosquitoes whined outside my netting.

I had a warm dry place to sleep, my belly was full, and I was in good company. Eladio's farm had reminded me that contentment can be found in simple things. In spite of the noise of the rain, the animals and my snoring friends, the cabin seemed calm and peaceful as I drifted off to sleep.

Watch Your Step

A rooster that wouldn't quit crowing had us moving as soon as the first light hit the treetops. It was one of those rare mornings with just a few drifting clouds and the promise of sunshine — not to be wasted. After a quick breakfast of bananas, I reorganized my insect-collecting gear. Eladio worked on his machete, filing a fresh, razor-sharp edge on it, and we headed off into the forest with Eladio leading the way.

Eladio was the perfect person to walk with in the jungle. He was silent, alert and skillful. He was able to find and cut a path with no apparent effort. His machete strokes were neat and economical, disposing of a vine here or a fallen branch there. It seemed as easy as walking. But I knew that his skill was based on years of practice and that it would take me twice as much time to cut a trail half as long.

Eladio opened up a trail into some of the wettest rain forest I had ever seen. Small streams poured down the steep slopes. Mushrooms and molds were sprouting on every fallen log. I even found insects coated with fungus. One of them was a large speckled weevil with a long snout. The weevil had actually been invaded by a fungus that spreads through its body, feeding on its tissues. Before the weevil dies this remarkable fungus somehow causes the weevil, normally a low-lying creature, to crawl to the very top of a palm leaf and clamp on in a tight death grip. Then the fungus bursts right out of the weevil, growing into a mushroom-like structure that opens to spread its infective spores on the breeze.

When we reached the Peñas Blancas River, Eladio headed upriver to cut more trail for another day's hike. Before I turned back I sat down for a rest on the river edge. The river was swollen with yesterday's rain and ripping along at high speed. I could hear the groaning of large rocks and boulders grinding and rolling under water along the riverbed. The water and gravity were working at the slow and endless task of wearing the mountain down, turning rock into gravel and gravel into sand, and carrying the sand to the lowlands and the ocean. I looked at the sand and gravel bar and thought how long it had taken to turn a huge boulder into fine sand. I thought about how long it had taken the river to carve the valley out of the mountain and how much time had gone into growing the great forest that blanketed the slopes. And I had so little time to see it all. I splashed cool clean river water in my face and headed back along the trail alone.

Along the streams, where the sun broke through, sun-loving plants like the heliconia grew in large clumps and produced tremendous stalks of flowers. I stood under one that reached from just above my head all the way down to my ankles.

It was easy to be entranced by the almost magical vegetation. I kept staring up, guessing at the height of tremendous trees, and I had to remind myself that this was a place where one had to walk very, very carefully.

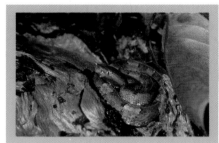

The warm lowland rain forest is home to a great variety of venomous snakes and stinging insects. Pit vipers, for example, thrive in warm wet jungles, and I soon saw a mottled green one coiled and camouflaged in some vegetation along the trail. It was warm enough here for the fer-de-lance, a large camouflaged snake that waits coiled beside game trails to ambush small mammals. One thing I wanted to avoid was a close encounter with one of these snakes.

Actually, I had to watch out for ants even more than for snakes. I knew that Eladio had lived down here for many years without once being bitten by a snake. But he had told me that he was always getting stung by ants and wasps.

Far Left: Heliconia flowers grow as long as an adult person. Above: Pit viper Right: Fer-de-lance, 2 m (6 ft) long

Some of these ants showed up in strange places. Along one section of trail near the river there were many cecropia trees with hollow stems that looked a bit like bamboo. When I tapped one stem, small azteca ants came boiling out of holes all along the trunk. They ran around furiously with their pointed back ends held straight up. When they reached my finger they swarmed all over it and began biting. Luckily their bite was irritating only on the soft skin between my fingers. But I could see that climbing a cecropia tree would be almost impossible because hundreds of these ants would swarm over my face and body.

The cecropia tree provides a home for the aztecas, and they aggressively attack any insect or animal they encounter on their tree. With the ants on duty, the tree stays free from grazing and leaf damage. To encourage this relationship, cecropia trees have hollow stems where the ants live. They also have special glandular areas that produce tiny white bits of a special protein-rich food for the ants.

For some reason large cecropias have few ants or no ants at all. Perhaps that is why the

three-toed sloths that love to eat cecropia leaves are usually seen in the largest cecropia trees, the ones that have lost the ant colonies.

At one point the trail skirted around a large fallen tree. The fallen tree had opened up a gap in the foliage, allowing sunlight to reach the forest floor, encouraging a dense growth of weedy plants. On these plants I found some green

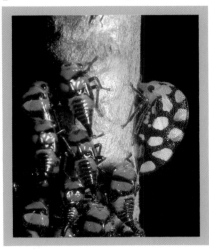

treehopper insects and some black and yellow polka-dotted ones. They had also developed a relationship with the ants. The hoppers were sucking sap out of plant stems, and the ants were walking all over the hoppers, milking the sweet sap from them. But the ants were working for their supper: when I poked at the treehoppers the ants rushed at my finger, biting wildly. The arrangement was something like dairy farming, with the treehoppers getting protection as they fed on the plant, and the ants getting sugary rewards for tending the hoppers.

Far Left: *Cecropia tree swarming with ants* Left: *Tree-hoppers being tended by ants* Above: *Polka-dotted treehopper adult and nymphs drinking sap*

But while I was watching all this, I found that I had stepped where I shouldn't have. Swarming up my pant leg, both inside and out, was a cloud of huge ants.

I was standing in the midst of an army ant raid! I jumped back along the trail, kicking off my boot and hiking up my pants. Only one large soldier ant, as big as a paperclip, had made its way onto my skin, but that was enough. It locked its great sickle-shaped mandibles into my calf and plunged its sting repeatedly into the skin. The fiery hot sting made me jump even higher.

When I yanked the army ant off my leg, I saw how determined its grip was. Its head remained firmly attached to my skin even when the rest of its body was broken off. I could see why South American Indians use these gripping army ant heads to stitch up open wounds.

I hastily brushed the remaining ants off my pants and boots and stepped back carefully to take a closer look at the raid. It was easy to do as long as I kept an eye on the shifting columns of ants spreading through the forest. At the head of the raid, scouts were dragging their abdomens along the ground and along branches, laying down a chemical signal to direct the other army ants to new areas and food sources. Sometimes to cross a gap they strung their bodies together in a chain so that other ants could run across from tree to tree. The endless columns of ants divided and criss-crossed and blended together again, always advancing, weaving their way up and across the forest.

Army ants carry off a wasp larva and, opposite, attack a scorpion.

Careful to keep out of their path (one army ant sting was more than enough), I gazed at the spectacle unfolding before me. The army of ants surged

forward. It was a tremendous feat of chemical coordination and communication among tens of thousands of individuals. Somehow all those ants, working without language or leaders, had managed to organize an effective hunt.

The impact of the hunt could be clearly heard and seen. The forest floor was crackling with activity as insects hopped and lizards scuttled

away, trying to flee the ants. I watched the ants mass-attack a scorpion. It struggled briefly, but the ants soon pinned it down securely and cut it to pieces. This was a hungry army.

I noticed that some insects and birds were actually following the ants. When katydids leaped up in the air to avoid the ants, large hairy tachinid flies, which had been swarming around, swooped in. Having spotted the katydids, they tried to lay their eggs on them. The fly maggots could then burrow in and feed on the katydids — that is, if the ants didn't find them first. Birds were using the same technique, swooping down to pick off insects scared up by the ants. They reminded me of seagulls following behind a tractor for worms.

Trailing the birds were hovering butterflies, delicate slow-flying varieties with long narrow wings. Some had glistening transparent wings like shining stained glass, and others were tiger-striped in orange and black. They were visiting leaves where birds had left droppings and sipping up the nutrients they needed to make butterfly eggs. So the legion of ants was not only eating its way through the forest; it was feeding another crowd of organisms as it went.

The sting of the army ant continued to throb as I hiked back to Eladio's house. I didn't appreciate the sting. But the ant was part of a great spectacle, and seeing it was worth the pain. Today I had seen yet again how the relationships among different plants and animals were vital strands woven together in a living forest.

Right: *Glasswing butterflies gather nutrients from bird droppings.* Far Right: *A hairy tachinid fly poised on a leaf*

Disappearing Places

It was almost time for me to leave. Once I got back to Monteverde, I would board a series of buses back to the airport, then my plane home to Canada.

As I trudged back toward Monteverde I thought about why the tropical jungle was disappearing. I passed Alejandro's cabin and stopped by the abandoned farmhouse to pick some oranges. Looking at those poor houses told me the answer. At the heart of it was human poverty and population pressure.

I was heading back to a cabin in Monteverde that was modest and simple. Yet it was a luxurious house compared with Eladio's place or Alejandro's. I had seen how hard Eladio worked.

Why should Eladio want or expect to live more poorly than we live? If living a better life meant cutting the forest down to raise cattle, almost anyone in Eladio's position would go ahead and cut.

Eladio had told me why he had first moved into the Peñas Blancas valley. All the farmland in the valley where he was born was already taken. More than half of it was owned by just one man. This imbalance meant there was nothing for people like Eladio, no matter how hard they worked. Even worse, the deforested land where Eladio was born was being farmed poorly. Instead of growing food crops for the local people, much of the land was feeding beef cattle for export to other countries.

Eladio's situation is typical of people all over the tropics. Agricultural development has destroyed the forest but has not really improved the lives of many people. For example, even though beef production has increased greatly in Costa Rica, much of the beef goes to other countries to feed people who already have more than enough food.

Costa Ricans now eat less beef than ever, while we gobble fast-food hamburgers by the ton. The cats and dogs of North America and Europe eat more beef than Costa Ricans do. So we have contributed directly to this destruction. The goods we consume often come from the tropics and cause the destruction of tropical forests.

The tropics seem far away from us, but parts of the tropics touch us every day. Anyone who has drunk coffee, tea, cola or orange juice has drunk a bit of the tropics. If you've eaten a chocolate bar, you've eaten a bit of a tropical forest tree. Your hamburger at a fast-food restaurant may have come from a tropical country. The sugar in your food, the bananas on your cereal, the cotton in your clothes all probably came from the tropics. The furniture in your house is often built from the wood of tropical trees.

Many of our most important medicines come from tropical plants and animals. A friend of mine, just a young man, recently became ill with cancer. Not long ago every person with this illness died from it. But my friend was completely cured with the help of a new anti-cancer drug. The drug is found only in a tropical flower. An important drug used all over the world in surgical operations was first discovered in the venom of a South American snake. Without research on the tropical plants and animals and protection for the forests, we could lose many precious medicines before they can be discovered.

Site of what once was lush tropical forest

76

There are many other examples of why the tropics are important. Many of the songbirds we enjoy seeing and hearing every summer migrate to the tropics every winter. Around Monteverde oven birds were common — the same

oven birds that I enjoy each summer in Ontario as their song "tea-cher, tea-cher" sounds through the pines and hemlocks. As their wintering habitats are destroyed, many of these migratory songbirds are starting to become extinct. In addition, the tropical forests protect soils from erosion and reduce flooding. The tropical forests also humidify and cool the warm tropical air and influence weather patterns all over the world. So it is possible that forest destruction might change the world's climate.

This does not mean we should stop eating bananas or drinking orange juice. But we should help tropical countries protect their precious rain forests. People from all over the world are now rallying to help save rain forests before they disappear forever.

When I got back to my cabin in Monteverde it was time to pack up and leave for home. The very next day I was on board a jet, ready to fly north. As the plane took off, it circled and then banked steeply over the green mountains.

I had traveled from the dry, dusty Pacific lowlands up to those lush mountain rain forests. In a few short weeks I'd explored the windswept cloud forest that straddles the backbone of the Americas, then slogged down into the steamy Atlantic jungle in the lowlands. I felt as if I had discovered a new world along the way.

Looking down I thought of the many beautiful plants and animals I had seen and the many more that remained to be discovered in the jungles below me. I took out my notebook and began planning my return. ◅

Afterword

There is a saying that 'Knowledge is Power'. If that is true, and I am inclined to believe that it is, we need all the knowledge about the natural environment we can lay our hands on if we are to have the power to prevent it being destroyed.

This book is full of information about the richness and variety of the tropical jungle, about how it works and about the threats to its future. If you have gained any knowledge from it, I suggest that you turn it into power by supporting one of the many organisations concerned with the conservation of nature and the natural environment.

HRH PRINCE PHILIP,
THE DUKE OF EDINBURGH

WINDSOR CASTLE

Index